A Little Book of
Thank Yous

A Little Book of
Thank Yous
Letters, Notes & Quotes

Addie Johnson

Conari
Press

CORAL GABLES

Cover Design: Elina Diaz
Cover Photo: stock.adobe.com/ floraldeco
Interior Layout Design: Elina Diaz

Published by Conari Press, an imprint of Mango Media Inc.

Page 94 contain an excerpt from "The Power of Gratitude" by Stephen
Post from the November 2007 issue of *Guideposts* magazine, reprinted
with permission.

For permission requests, please contact the publisher at:
Mango Publishing Group
2850 Douglas Road, 2nd Floor
Coral Gables, FL 33134 USA
info@mango.bz

For special orders, quantity sales, course adoptions and corporate sales,
please email the publisher at sales@mango.bz. For trade and wholesale
sales, please contact Ingram Publisher Services at customer.service@
ingramcontent.com or +1.800.509.4887.

A Little Book of Thank Yous: Letters, Notes & Quotes

ISBN: (p) 978-1-64250-427-9 (e) 978-1-64250-428-6
BISAC: SEL021000, SELF-HELP / Motivational & Inspirational
LCCN: 2020940925

Table of Contents

Foreword

The book you are holding in your hands exemplifies the expression, "small but mighty."

On the surface, *A Little Book of Thank Yous* by Addie Johnson looks like a simple and sweet book.

Which it is.

But it *also* packs a potent and powerful punch.

This book, if you let it, can change your life.

Actually, let me rephrase that: this book, if you *use* it, *will* change your life.

I trust that you noticed the change from the passive "let it" to active "use it." And that you also let yourself feel not just the *possibility* of change, but the *certainty*.

These are no small things.

You can read this book and enjoy the beautiful quotes and stories. You can delight in Addie's creative ideas. You can nod, knowingly, at the encouragements, which you sense would make a difference if you followed them.

But what I'm asking you, on your own behalf and that of anyone you love, is to please make this book a mighty force in your life by not just reading it, but by putting it into practice.

Make the commitment right now to read this book with a pen and some sticky notes at the ready; annotate as you read. Keep in mind that you aren't just taking notes, you're making a gratitude action plan!

Make notes about which ideas you want to try right away and for whom. Make notes about specific people that drop into your mind whom you want to thank. Make notes of creative twists that will transform Addie's ideas into oh-so-personal gratitudes of your own.

And while you are making all the notes, pause every once and a while to feel the joy pulsing through your body. Because one of the beautiful secrets about gratitude is that simply thinking of it changes our state of mind!

"Hey, wait a minute," you might be saying. "If simply *thinking* about gratitude will make me feel good, why can't I simply read this book, feel great, then put it on the shelf when I'm finished? What's the need for that gratitude action plan you are talking about?"

I'm so glad you asked!

Reading and thinking about gratitude will make you feel good. There's no doubt that you will put this book down feeling better than before you started.

However, what Addie knows from her experience and what I know from my own gratitude practices is that gratitude in action creates a long-lasting ripple of love, connection, and joy. Gratitude in action shifts your outlook, your energy, your relationships, and your sense of self.

There is an exponential effect that happens when we go from *thinking about* gratitude to *acting with* gratitude.

Here's a simple example. Let's say you feel happy thinking about the barista at your favorite café and the way she always greets you with a warm hello and remembers that you like a shot of vanilla in your latte. That feels good to think about, sure.

But if you put that gratitude into action and you write a positive and thankful letter to the owner of the café where your happy barista works, here's what's possible:

- While you are writing the thank-you letter, you are prolonging the good feeling. As Rick Hanson, author of *Buddha's Brain* says, "The brain is like Velcro for negative experiences and Teflon for positives ones." He says we can help overcome the negativity bias of the brain by spending more time focusing on the positive. This "hardwires" happiness. Writing that letter, rather than just a thinking about it, will help teach your body to feel good.

- When the owner of the café receives your letter about that excellent barista, the owner will feel grateful and happy. Customers are more likely to complain than to compliment. This will be a wonderful uplift.

- The café owner will likely show the letter to the barista, who will feel so pleased that her positivity is having an impact in the world. She may have been having a hard day. A letter like this could turn it all around and make her feel buoyant again.

- The next time you visit the café, you will have a new (deeper) connection to the barista and to the owner. Perhaps you'll pause to talk for a few minutes longer. Perhaps she'll let you know how grateful she was that you sent that positive note to her employer. Maybe you will remind each other that the small things (like her cheery welcome or your handwritten note) make a huge difference.

- Something new—shared gratitude—is connecting you to your café. When you walk in, there's a new layer of joy just waiting for you. There's been a long-lasting shift, resulting in more good feelings!

That's just one example of the ripple effects of gratitude in action.

I've been practicing many forms of gratitude and learning new ways to say "thank you" for the last three decades of my life. I've experienced those ripple effects, what I call "the circle of giving and receiving" time and time again.

I've never met Addie Johnson, but I bet that if I passed her on the street today, she'd have a big smile on her face. I bet that her devotion to "thank you" has transformed her life. I bet she'd nod knowingly and say out loud (just like she does later in this book) "The more you give, the more you get."

You've got what you need to guide you to a life filled with gratitude in your hands. Follow Addie's formula and, before you know it, you'll be walking down the street with a wide smile on your face and a skip in your step.

I promise.

—Sherry Richert Belul, founder of Simply Celebrate and author of *Say It Now: 33 Creative Ways to Say I LOVE YOU to the Most Important People in Your Life*

P.S. Thank you, Addie, for creating a little book that has had a *big* impact on me. And thank you, dear reader, for your desire to feel and share more gratitude. The world desperately needs all it can get. I'm grateful!

Introduction

"If the only prayer you ever say in your entire life is 'thank you,' it will be enough."
—Meister Eckhart

THANK YOU. How many times a day do you say it? How many times a day do you mean it? From a most commonplace "thank you" to a stranger on the street, to the most exalted thanks we send up to the heavens, I know of no other phrase that is more useful, more versatile, more uncomplicated, more soothing, or more potent.

Our word "gratitude" comes from the Latin *gratus*, which means both thankful and pleasing. To give thanks is to get pleasure. It is linked to our word "grace," both in the sense of general elegance and beauty and in the sense of one of our highest ideals, that state of grace in which we are closest to divinity. It is linked to community and propriety in the sense of our graciousness to one another. Gratitude encircles us in a perpetual cycle of giving and receiving, multiplying our gifts as we offer them and enriching us as we give.

There are those lucky moments when we feel soaring gratitude, a thankfulness that envelopes all measures and seasons—an appreciation for the smallest things all the way up to the very fact of life in the universe and touching on everything in between. It's a wonderful feeling, but it can be pitifully short lived. As much as I would like to live in this state of grace, I spend the vast majority of my days in the opposite state—grumpy, tired, even downright ungrateful. When I realize I'm in that kind of funk, I sometimes try to force myself into thankfulness whenever and wherever I think it might be good for me, as though gratitude were some strong, bitter tonic that will clear the sourness out of my heart and the trouble out of my life on demand. As you can imagine, I've had pretty limited success with that.

As children, we thank when prompted. But a child's genuine gratitude is communicated far in advance of the prodding to say the words "thank you." The eyes widen, the face turns to yours, and a moment of wonderment is shared and expressed nonverbally. The thanks do not correlate to how expensive the gift was, nor to how much effort or thought you put into it. Something as small as a lollipop might get the biggest response. But because we have a custom, we press the child to say the words, and they become an afterthought, a duty, even a chore. As an adult, gratitude loses its meaning and its strength the moment it becomes something we feel we ought to do rather than something we delight in doing.

This book is a collection of ways to rediscover the joy of gratitude, to extend those moments of passionate connection and thankfulness into the tiniest everyday details and the overreaching relationships and themes of life. It's a collage of quotes, notes, and thoughts about gratitude itself as well as ideas and ways to put it into action through words and deeds.

The simplest of these is of course the key to it all: *Thank you.* That's it. Two words; it couldn't be simpler. Gratitude lives and breathes through expression, and as Gertrude Stein said, "Silent gratitude isn't very much use to anyone." Say it, write it, intone it, whisper it, sing it: from quick, meaningful expressions of thanks to a thank you through actions as much as through words, to an out-of-the-blue thank you for someone you love, to an exaltation of everything wonderful that you lift up and out of yourself. Every chance you have, in any moment of the day. *Thank you. Thank you. Thank you.*

Chapter One

Giving, Gratitude, and Grace— A Way of Life

"Happiness cannot be traveled to, owned, earned, worn, or consumed. Happiness is the spiritual experience of living every minute with love, grace, and gratitude."

–Denis Waitley

I catch myself sometimes thinking that these three g's—giving, gratitude, and grace—are like extra credit in life, meaning they're a wonderful bonus once I get through the other stuff: obligations, stress, difficulty, trying to find some way to be happy as the skies seem to be darkening around me. It can be easy to forget, particularly if I'm having a tough time, that those three g's are the pith and center of life, not things to shove to the outskirts of my attention. Giving is always possible, no matter how scarce my resources. Gratitude isn't just an afterthought, it's a forethought (as well as a during thought!) and one that enriches the good times and sustains me through the bad. Grace is a goal and an inspiration and can be found in everything from the most mundane to the most exciting moments and everywhere in between. There are so many wonderful small ways to put these into practice: as we express our thanks for the gifts we receive, as we dream up the wonderful gifts we can give to others, as we practice the spirit of graceful living in every way we can. More of these three g's will bring the kind of life I want to grab hold of and never let go.

"We make a living by what we get, we make a life by what we give."
—Sir Winston Churchill

We're all trying to make a life in the best way we know. It isn't easy, and in the process we may well lose sight of what we really want and need. Or we may lose track of other people's wants and needs in the relentless pursuit of our own. We try our best to make a living, getting more whenever and however we can, while making sacrifices and difficult choices along the way. Sometimes we delay the giving we might be inclined to do, whether it's to charity, more time to spend with our kids, or putting time and energy toward our own passions. We put off giving until we feel we have made enough of a living, as though crossing the threshold of some magic number or career milestone will suddenly make us feel inclined to generosity. Are we waiting until we have something to spare before we give anything? There is a way to make a life by giving, giving, giving, and it may not be any easier, but it will most certainly be more fulfilling.

"Love is, above all, the gift of oneself."
—Jean Anouilh

Gratitude is love. Love is gratitude. An expression of love is an expression of gratitude. I love you means, in part, I am grateful that you are in my life. I am grateful that I get the gift of getting to share my love with you. And any thank you is an expression of love.

"If we have the opportunity to be generous with our hearts, ourselves, we have no idea of the depth and breadth of love's reach."
—Margaret Cho

Thank You for Appreciating Me

This is a thank you for a thank you and is often overlooked. When you get to the end of your rope, doing and doing for everyone else in your life, hearing a thank you can break the dam of pent-up emotions. Knowing that someone appreciates what you're doing can lift a terrific burden and is a gift in and of itself. One good turn deserves another. Sending a thank you in the form of a note or an email, or just a phone call, can mean the world.

Thank You for Being Who You Are

It takes courage to be who you really are, especially if you are not quite like everyone else around. That courage can be contagious in a wonderful way. I have a friend who was a complete outcast in high school. She didn't even really understand why, except that she's a firecracker and someone who doesn't see any point in changing her looks, mannerisms, or beliefs to fit the status quo. A lot of high schoolers devote themselves to changing their looks, mannerisms, or beliefs in order to fit in, and no one knew what to make of my friend, so they ridiculed and excluded her. She got a letter years later from one of her classmates, and part of it was about thanking her for having the strength and conviction to be who she was, while not trying to change or fit in for the sake of it. It turns out that my friend's struggle was being watched more closely than she imagined, and that this classmate had gone on to find the same strength in herself and was so much the better for it.

"Give what you have. To someone, it may be better than you dare to think."
—Henry Wadsworth Longfellow

I've read quite a bit about one of the most successful modes of philanthropy out there right now—the idea of micro loans. Given mostly to individual women or groups of women, the loans of as little as a couple of dollars are usually used as seed money for a business, buying starter supplies to build a store, or beginning a weaving or crafts collective. The success rates are huge, and there are all sorts of added benefits for the families of the women involved, like improved nutrition and education for the children. So, even while we feel like we're desperately struggling in a richer nation, those couple of dollars we keep in the penny jar might be able to do something somewhere. In a broader sense, we need to remember not to censor our own generosity for fear that we don't have enough to give. Giving what you have is the best you can do, and it can make all the difference.

Thank you for giving what you have.

"It is expressly at those times when we feel needy that we will benefit the most from giving."

–Ruth Ross

Thank you for being there.

"My misery loved your company. Thank you for being there!"

—Unknown

Thank you for giving me hope.

Thanks for giving it your all.

Thank you for helping me through a difficult time.

Thank you for teaching by example.

Thank you for calming my fears.

Thank you for inspiring me to go on when I felt
like I couldn't make it.

"To give without any reward, or any notice, has a special quality of its own."

–Anne Morrow Lindbergh

"I would like to believe when I die that I have given myself away like a tree that sows seeds every spring and never counts the loss, because it is not loss, it is adding to future life. It is the tree's way of being. Strongly rooted perhaps, but spilling out its treasure on the wind."

—May Sarton

Expressing gratitude serves as one of the most moving condolences I know. When my father died, I got a letter from one of his best friends with memories of their youth together. His appreciation for my father—his dumb jokes, his adventurous spirit, even his stubbornness—came through so clearly, and I read the note again and again, feeling wrapped in the love his friend had for him, and it was a huge comfort.

"Gratitude is the fairest blossom which springs from the soul."
—Henry Ward Beecher

Giving flowers as a thank you means so much. They reflect back the sweetness of any good deed—they brighten any room and bring the natural world indoors and closer to us. From the simplest single stem rose to the most luxurious bouquet, you just can't go wrong. Give dark-pink roses or campanula (also known as bellflower) for gratitude, pink roses for grace, and lavender for devotion.

Out-of-the-Blue Thank You!

Isn't it wonderful to get an unexpected gift? A care package from your best friend, a card from someone just to say they're thinking of you, a single rose from someone you love. It's just as thrilling to get a thank you out of the blue. When's the last time you got to thank a friend, parent, child, teacher, coworker, or anyone else for something they do every day or simply for being who they are?

Thank You, Whoever You Are

How do you thank an anonymous donor? Write a thank you and post it where they might see it—on the Internet or in a public place. It might be a picture made with the art supplies donated to the class, or it can be something done in turn anonymously to pass the giving on to someone else. But always remember what any anonymous giver knows: the giving itself is a great reward, and the fact that you benefited from the gift is, in itself, an expression of your gratitude.

Mr. Volkmar von Fuehlsdorff
German Consulate General
3450 Wilshire Boulevard
Los Angeles, California

Dear Mr. von Fuehlsdorff:

Thank you for your champagne.
It arrived, I drank it and I was gayer.
Thanks again.

My best,
Marilyn Monroe

"Gratitude is not only the greatest of virtues, but the parent of all others."

—Cicero

"Feeling gratitude and not expressing it is like wrapping a present and not giving it."

—William Arthur Ward

"The fragrance always remains in the hand that gives the rose."

—Heda Bejar

Thank you for being my friend...

"Blessed are they who have the gift of making friends, for it is one of God's best gifts. It involves many things, but above all, the power of going out of one's self and appreciating whatever is noble and loving in another."

–Thomas Hughes

Thank you for the gift...

"The great art of giving consists in this: the gift should cost very little and yet be greatly coveted, so that it may be the more highly appreciated."

—Baltasar Gracián

It's just what I needed right now...

"The excellence of a gift lies in its appropriateness rather than in its value."

—Charles Dudley Warner

I can hardly wait to return the favor...

"You try to give away
what you want yourself."

—Lois McMaster Bujold

"The best thing to give to your enemy is forgiveness; to an opponent, tolerance; to a friend, your heart; to your child, a good example; to a father, deference; to your mother, conduct that will make her proud of you; to yourself, respect; to all men, charity."

—Francis Maitland Balfour

"Life is the first gift,
love is the second,
and understanding
the third."
—Marge Piercy

"The dedicated life is
the life worth living.
You must give with your
whole heart."
—Annie Dillard

The Currency of Gratitude...

Pennies

flowers picked from your garden
a sticky note on the fridge
chocolate, chocolate, chocolate

Nickels

a bottle of wine of a meaningful vintage
a scrapbook of collected photos and remembrances a
donation to a favorite charity
a poem or song you wrote for the occasion

Silver dollars

your firstborn child (well, maybe not...)

jewelry (speaking of firstborn children, in some circles it's
customary for a new father to give a piece of jewelry to a new
mother—a push present!)

a memento requested from a particular hero (I knew a teacher
once who wrote to her student's favorite baseball star and
presented him with a signed card from him as a thank you
for surpassing the high standard she had set for him) a trip
someplace special—just to dinner, or a longer trip to a
meaningful place

A Thank You to a Teacher...

Dear Agelio,

I have thought of writing this letter for fifteen years, and I am just now doing it. I didn't ever mean to wait that long, and I'm hoping by some miracle that what I want to say has percolated long enough that I'll be able to say it in as clear and strong a way as I feel it.

I just found this quote, by Carl Jung:

> An understanding heart is everything in a teacher and cannot be esteemed highly enough. One looks back with appreciation to the brilliant teachers, but with gratitude to those who touched our human feeling. The curriculum is so much necessary raw material, but warmth is the vital element for the growing plant and for the soul of the child.

I remember very clearly a lot of what you taught me, down to the details of exercises and assignments, which seems pretty crazy to me since I don't have very clear memories of a lot of my time in high school, especially the year or so after my dad died.

I feel so lucky to have gotten to spend time in your classroom learning in a way that had more to do with life and art, and learning to really see, more than almost any other class I got to take. It was as if you sat down and wrote a curriculum that said:

Learn to take photographic portraits of young artists.

Learn to play the guitar your father gave you.

Learn to see things like an artist sees them.

Grieve some.

I feel like you gave so freely of the "understanding heart" that Jung's talking about in such a simple, unpretentious, chill way, and I've thought about that a lot over the past fifteen years, in becoming a theatre artist, running a theatre company, writing, and being a mom. I really can't thank you enough for that, and I just wanted you to know how much it meant to me then and still means to me now.

I hope all's well in your life and your work and that you and your family are doing great.

With huge respect and much love,

Addie

No matter what your spiritual or religious inclination, sending your praise toward the heavens or out into the universe brightens your outlook and lifts up your soul.

"Wake at dawn with a winged heart and give thanks for another day of loving."

—Kahlil Gibran

"We give thanks for unknown blessings already on their way."

—Sacred ritual chant

"God gave you a gift of 86,400 seconds today. Have you used one to say 'thank you'?"

—William Arthur Ward

"Every time we remember to say 'thank you,' we experience nothing less than heaven on earth."

—Sarah Ban Breathnach

"To the generous mind the heaviest debt is that of gratitude, when it is not in our power to repay it."

—Benjamin Franklin

"The glorious gifts of
the gods are not to be
cast aside."

–Homer

"If you can give your
son or daughter
only one gift, let it
be Enthusiasm."

–Bruce Barton

Chapter Two

The Power of Words, the Wonder of Deeds

"As we express our gratitude, we must never forget that the highest appreciation is not to utter words, but to live by them."

—John Fitzgerald Kennedy

In the daily practice of gratitude, we have so many options. Finding the thanks that fits the gesture is a fine art—whether it's through words over the phone or handwritten in a note, or by the return of a gift or favor, or something in action alone that conveys the spirit of thanks—there are myriad ways to express ourselves. We can challenge ourselves to find the truest, strongest way to say thanks, and to always remember that the highest appreciation we can offer is to use our gifts to the fullest as we go about our day-to-day lives and as we apply our moral values to the overall course of our life path. Write a thank-you note, throw an appreciation party, celebrate in unexpected ways, and live in a spirit of thankfulness.

"Letters mingle souls." —John Donne

Handwritten letters in script or printed in block letters. Typed emails. Sticky notes on the fridge or in a lunch box. Every time we put our thoughts down and send them off to be read by someone else, we call on the alchemy of hearts and minds joining through simple ink and paper. We remember how we are connected; we feel the mingling of our souls. It's powerful magic, available to us whenever we want it.

Ways to Say Thank You

In your own handwriting, and with your own words:

- buy a lovely card

- write an email, personalizing it with special fonts and graphics

- take out an ad in your local newspaper

- take the time to say it in person, especially over a cup of coffee or a meal

- talk on the phone

- send the thanks through a twist on the game of telephone—so that the intended recipient of your thanks' ears are buzzing as they hear how grateful you are from everyone, they know

Things You Can Make

On the more traditional side:

- Photo albums and scrapbooks.

- Baking cookies or a cake made at home always taste better, even if they're from a box!

- A flower arrangement you made yourself.

- Handmade cards—one of my favorite simple ideas is to cut a stencil of a heart shape out of a coffee can lid, and kids can color it in to make a design on the front of the card.

- Handicrafts: knitting, origami, décolletage, etc.

Not so traditional:

- Send a copy of your letter to a superior. I recently read this comment from a physician who felt like this about writing thank-you notes to doctors: "Finally, I agree that a letter to a person's employer or boss is usually the best gift a person can receive, physician or otherwise. In my case, please also send a copy to my mother."

- Videos—you can do something simple and sweet on your home computer and post it online for everyone to see.

- You can make a Twitter, Facebook, or other social networking thank you, or create a viral email campaign just to send on your gratitude.

- Appreciation buttons—this is a great one for a teacher, to come into a class full of students wearing thank-you buttons made just for them!

- A thank-you singing telegram—order one through a service, hire the acapella group from a local college, or organize your friends and do your own.

Things You Can Do

Traditional:

- Take the person out to dinner

- Offer to return the favor and follow through as soon as you get the chance

- Send coffee, wine, or gift cards

- Give sauna/massage/salon gift certificates

- Chip in with others to do something special the person wouldn't otherwise be able to afford or get to do

Not so traditional:

- Personalize something—T-shirts, baseball caps, candles, scents, bath salts

- Tattoo, temporary tattoo, or other body art such as henna or body paint

- Learn how to say thank you in the person's native language, or in a way that's traditional in their own culture

- Graffiti a thank you in shaving cream or chalk outside someone's door

- Surprise someone by traveling a long distance to say thank you in person

- Skywriting—why not?

- Pay it forward—pass the gift on in an innovative way, and write a letter or make a phone call with all the juicy details

"Generosity is giving more than you can, and pride is taking less than you need."

—Kahlil Gibran

"Sow good services; sweet remembrances will grow from them."

—Madame de Staël

"Gratitude is when memory is stored in the heart and not in the mind."

—Lionel Hampton

"No duty is more urgent than that of returning thanks."
–St. Ambrose

One of the early lessons we all get about thank-you notes is that sooner is better. Do it now, while you're still thinking of it. And yes, late is better than nothing at all, but try to keep in mind what getting a handwritten thank-you card means to the giver—you don't want to delay that joy. It is so satisfying when you've given something to receive the acknowledgment, especially if the gift was sent across a long distance. Picking up the phone is great, emailing is wonderful, and I don't know about you, but there's something in me that still thrills like a little kid at the thought of a handwritten letter—it makes my heart jump a bit when I open the mailbox. There's something magical about it, getting a letter with your name on it. Remember that and don't delay—put your thanks into the world right away.

Other Tips for Thank-You Notes

Make the writing fun for yourself. I'm a sucker for a beautiful pen and nice paper, and I have a special stash to write letters and notes with.

Be specific. We all love juicy details.

Write it like you'd say it. I sometimes catch myself in formal mode with thank yous, and it doesn't have to be that way. Start by saying what you mean out loud, as if the person were there with you. Write that down as a rough draft, and if it needs a few tweaks to make sense on the page, by all means edit it, but starting with your own words always makes it better.

Keep stationery on hand of all different sizes. You don't always want or need to write a lot, and two or three sentences can look a bit silly floating in white space, so fit the note to the need.

Time for the Baby

I recently went to a baby shower where people wrote out their own envelopes for thank-you cards, and I thought it was a wonderful idea. No one wants a pile of thank yous to be a burden on a new mom—that's silly. But of course, she wants to express how she feels, and what an easy way to collect addresses that also makes the task faster and easier for her. She was able to focus on expressing how she felt, pop it in the pre-addressed envelope, and get back to the baby.

"To write a thank-you letter was no big deal in our house. 'Tell them all about our Christmas,' my mother would say, sure in the knowledge that we would tell it well and in detail and that everyone would be fascinated. Irish people are inclined to write long letters, as if it is a matter of huge importance that no detail be left unexplained."

—Maeve Binchy

Henry Ford received this letter, presumably from half of the legendary pair of outlaws Bonnie and Clyde. No one's ever been able to prove it came from him for sure, but Ford wrote back a thank-you letter that Clyde never saw—he'd moved on from Tulsa and six weeks later was killed by a barrage of police bullets while sitting at the wheel of a stolen V8 Ford.

Tulsa Okla
10th April
Mr. Henry Ford
Detroit Mich.

Dear Sir:

While I still have got breath in my lungs, I will tell you what a dandy car you make. I have drove Fords exclusively when I could get away with one. For sustained speed and freedom from trouble the Ford has got ever other car skinned and even if my business hasn't been strictly legal it don't hurt anything to tell you what a fine car you got in the V8.

Yours truly,
Clyde Champion Barrow

"It's a sign of mediocrity when you demonstrate gratitude with moderation."
—Roberto Benigni

I get embarrassed saying thank you sometimes and especially accepting thanks. When I lived in Italy, I was corrected by the mother in the family I stayed with. She pointed out that whenever anybody said thank you to me, "Grazie," I replied "Fa niente," meaning "it's nothing." She explained that I ought to say "Prego," which means "you're welcome." I was a little annoyed and honestly didn't think there was much of a difference, certainly not enough to worry about. But in thinking about it more, and many times since, it makes so much sense. "It's nothing" was my way of trying to minimize my discomfort with thank you, but it ended up minimizing the experience and belittling the thanks. Thank you is important, and so is you're welcome!

Please and Thank You

My friend Jan inspired me with her fun way of teaching my toddler to enjoy saying those polite phrases. When he'd ask for something, instead of saying "what do you say?" or "what's the magic word?" in a leading way, she'd say "ooh, ooh, what do you get to say?" in a really excited way, like she was ready to start a little play with wonderful dialogue. He'd smile and shout "please" and she'd pretend to be bowled over by the delivery. Then when he got what he wanted she'd again prompt him for his line—he'd say "thank you!" and she'd say "now what do I get to say?" and he'd say it with her, loud and clear, "you're welcome!" Big smiles all around, and the memory of having fun just saying please, thank you, and you're welcome.

When I sat down to write a card to my mother for her sixtieth birthday, I realized that what I had to say wouldn't even begin to fit. I was thinking of the poems and lists that she has often written for me on the occasion of my birthday or another important event, a card that was a gift in itself in the beauty of its words and insights. So, I settled on a list, "sixty things worth celebrating, or that you gave me, or that I am thankful for," and called it simply: thoughts for my mama on her sixtieth birthday. The list included:

- writing poems or stories for me on birthdays (or lists— like this one!)

- that you like to go off-roading in a Jeep and that seems out of character

- day trips, weekend trips, trips to the grocery store

- an old, old audiotape of us singing songs in the car when I was very little

- a well-intoned "oh sh*t!"

- a love of popcorn for dinner

- words, words, words

- poetry, poetry, poetry

- singing off-key

- freedom to troop around on my own as a kid (even if I did get myself deep into ravines and far into drainage sewers)

- knowing that you'll always be there, and that you'll always listen

and it concluded like this, still in list form:

- and here's to the future—

- blessings raining down on you forever and ever—

- adventure, love, laughter, health, family, challenge, joy, work, and play

- with all of us, who love you so.

Thank You for Being There for Me.

> "One joy shatters a hundred griefs."
> –Chinese proverb

Thank you for sharing.

> "What we have done for ourselves alone dies with us; what we have done for others and the world remains and is immortal."
> –Albert Pike

Thank you for showing me an example of how to live.

"Somebody saw something in you once—and that is partly why you're where you are today. Find a way to thank them."

—Don Ward

Thank you for letting me go.

"Truly loving another means letting go of all expectations. It means full acceptance, even celebration of another's personhood."

—Karen Casey

Thank you for enriching my life.

"We can only be said to be alive in those moments when our hearts are conscious of our treasures."

–Thornton Wilder

Thanks for having me.

"Hospitality: a little fire, a little food, and an immense quiet."
—Ralph Waldo Emerson

Thank you for inspiring me.

"Families are the compass that guide us. They are the inspiration to reach great heights, and our comfort when we occasionally falter."
–Brad Henry

Thank you for talking it through with me.

"You can disagree without being disagreeable."
–Zig Ziglar

The six most important words— "I admit I made a mistake."

The five most important words—"You did a good job."

The four most important words— "What is your opinion?"

The three most important words—"If you please..."

The two most important words—"Thank you!"

The one most important word—"We."

The least important word—"I."

—Unknown

No Exaggerations Necessary

Ever get a thank you that's a bit over the top? No one needs to pretend that the gift of a sweater, a check to help with expenses that first year of college, or the opportunity to come in for a job interview was an earth-shattering event. Tune in to what really mattered to you in the gift, even if it doesn't seem like the most effusive praise, and put it in your own words even if it's not grammatically correct (unless of course it's written to your English teacher!). The more appropriate the thanks is to the gift or the occasion and the more detailed and personal the response, the better.

Your Perspective

I recently read an article by baseball star Doug Glanville in which he talked about finally going through the mountain of mail that he'd collected over the last years of his career. He was determined to read—and, when possible, respond to—everything, and of this experience he said, "the fun part was being able to paint a picture of my entire career through the eyes of others. People remembered the most subtle moments. There was the story of a man who was wearing a halo following an automobile accident. I threw a ball to him before the game in an effort to lift his spirits, and, after overshooting him, I went back and threw him another baseball, this one landing softly in his hands. His wife took the time to write me a thank-you letter."

Glanville's article made me remember that we often forget the power of our own perspective, particularly if we are writing to someone we hugely admire. Just telling it like we see it as we say thank you is more moving than any flowery or overblown language could ever be.

On December 29, 1943, English prime minister Winston Churchill wrote a thank-you letter to be published in newspapers around the world as he recovered from a bout of pneumonia during the war. He describes in newsy detail the days and weeks of his illness, reporting on the medicine prescribed to him and detailing his physician's thoughts and actions. He writes, "I thought that some of those who have been so kind as to inquire or express themselves in friendly terms about me would like to have this personal note from me, which they will please take as conveying my sincere thanks." What a wonderful thank you from one of the world's greatest leaders—to respond to personal, heartfelt concern about his health in kind with personal details, almost like those you might expect from a member of your own family, reassuring even as he expresses his intimate thanks on a grand scale.

"Gratitude is one of the least articulate of the emotions, especially when it is deep."
—Felix Frankfurter

How come it's easier to say thank you to a waiter bringing you a cup of coffee than to someone for saving your life? We expect so much of ourselves and each other when it comes to saying we're thankful, and yet the more important it is and the more intensely we feel it, the harder it is to express.

"Too great haste to repay an obligation is a kind of ingratitude."
–François de la Rochefoucauld

Enjoying, lingering, and accepting are parts of gratitude. If we rush to be grateful in some outward way that proves something, or if we feel the gift is a burden or a favor that must be returned or a wrong to be righted, the end result is a loss of joy for the receiver and the giver.

We underestimate the power of keeping in touch as a way to thank the people who helped us get where we are today. For a teacher, a parent, a mentor, or even a former boss, just knowing what you're up to is huge thanks and can be very gratifying. Take the time to let them know that their help made all the difference and to show them what you've made of yourself. Let them share in the pride of what you've accomplished. You can write this kind of thank-you note even if this person has passed away. It can be passed on to their loved ones as a remembrance of them, or just writing it out for yourself can remind you of how much you have to be grateful for.

"The spirit in which a thing is given determines that in which the debt is acknowledged; it's the intention, not the face-value of the gift, that's weighed."

—Seneca

Uh-oh

It may not be hard to find the perfect turn of phrase to thank someone for a gift you love, but what about the panic you feel when you just plain don't like it? What do you say that will not offend? What can you do that stays sincere and respectful?

"The greatest gift is a portion of thyself."
—Ralph Waldo Emerson

One of my all-time favorite presents I heard about from a friend: for Mother's Day one year, her nine-year-old daughter gave her a handmade booklet of coupons, each one for a different gift of time or energy for her mom. Some were practical, like "good for one (extra) night of doing the dishes." Some were whimsical: "good for one made-up song about anything you want it to be." And some were sweet: "good for one day of hanging out together and doing whatever you want to do."

A cheap, simple, lovely gift that expresses gratitude in the giving. Clearly this mom had given something of herself, as Emerson says, and the daughter was following suit. What a lovely exchange.

Focus on the thought and effort that went into the gift, and steer clear of specifics about the thing itself: "Knowing you were there and/or thought of me right now meant so much."

Pick an aspect of it that you do like and can talk about honestly—color, the feel of the fabric, the fact that it is handmade.

If possible, try not to say it was "unique" or "different"—I don't know about your family, but in mine those are code words for "I hate it."

Focus on your relationship and mention something you're looking forward to doing together in the future so that your note ends with something positive.

And Beware...

Gift receipts can be a trap! They are so standard now in certain stores that you may get a present that comes with one from someone who you know would probably be quite hurt if you exchanged their gift for something else. You have a few options:

Toss the receipt, find something lovely to say to the giver by way of thanks for the gift—you know they don't want you to return it, so don't be tempted.

If it's something with sizes, you can always try mentioning that it didn't fit and they didn't have one that did and you found something else wonderful to remember them by (this one depends on your taste for little white lies).

Regift it to someone who really would love it (and who lives far enough away for it not to be noticed).

Make a note of it—sometimes people who belly flop on the gifts they give us are buying for themselves. I'm guilty of this myself. I won't say I've gone so far as buying my non-cooking husband a set of pots and pans, but close... So, if that seems like it might be the case, you can always use the opportunity to write down or remember that preference for the next time you get a gift for that person.

Why not say thank you for a good deed by spreading it on and extending the generosity into the future? The idea of paying it forward, or repaying a debt by passing the gift on to someone new rather than back to the original giver, is at least as old as Benjamin Franklin, who said, "I do not pretend to give such a Sum; I only lend it to you. When you…meet with another honest Man in similar Distress, you must pay me by lending this Sum to him; enjoining him to discharge the Debt by a like operation, when he shall be able, and shall meet with another opportunity. I hope it may thus go thro' many hands, before it meets with a Knave that will stop its Progress. This is a trick of mine for doing a deal of good with a little money."

"One can never pay in gratitude; one can pay 'in kind' somewhere else in life."

—Anne Morrow Lindbergh

Chapter Three

Everyday Thank Yous, Lifelong Wellness

"Gratitude is a vaccine,
an antitoxin, and
an antiseptic."

–John Henry Jowett

"Hem your blessings with thank fulness so they don't unravel."

—Anonymous

"Thank you, God, for this good life and forgive us if we do not love it enough."

—Garrison Keillor

There is a mountain of scientific research that proves that one of the simplest ways to be happier, and even healthier, is to give thanks. Write down five things every night that you are grateful for. A daily practice of gratitude is a comfort, a tonic, and a lifeline. It connects you to the things and people that mean the most to you. It reminds you of what is real and worthy and plain old good about your life. And gratitude breeds more to be grateful for; taking the time to focus on the upside for ten minutes a day has the power to bring in more of the same. It might be the simplest thing you've ever added to your daily regimen and the shortest road to lifelong well-being and unmatched bliss.

"You must give some time to your fellow men. Even if it's a little thing, do something for others—something for which you get no pay but the privilege of doing it."

—Albert Schweitzer

A grateful heart is a giving heart, and a giving heart knows true grace.

"To our friends who have become family and our family who have become friends—May you be blessed with the same love and care you've given us."

—Mary Maude Daniels

Five Ideas for Everyday Expressions of Gratitude

Write in a journal—articulate what you're thankful for in story form as though you're writing a script or a novel. Get all the juicy details on paper or record them on tape.

Use your manners—remind yourself to amp up the thank yous all day long, for little things and big things. Be sincere about it and say it loud and proud!

Send a note—put something in the mail today to someone you appreciate.

Thank yourself—don't forget to recognize your own gifts.

Give back—doing for others really can be an expression of gratitude.

The Power of Gratitude

Researcher and professor of bioethics Stephen Post's studies have shown that love-related qualities—like gratitude—actually make us physically healthier.

Gratitude Defends. Just fifteen minutes a day focusing on the things you're grateful for will significantly increase your body's natural antibodies.

Gratitude Sharpens. Naturally grateful people are more focused mentally and measurably less vulnerable to clinical depression.

Gratitude Calms. A grateful state of mind induces a physiological state called resonance that's associated with healthier blood pressure and heart rate.

Gratitude Strengthens. Caring for others is draining. But grateful caregivers are healthier and more capable than less grateful ones.

Gratitude Heals. Recipients of donated organs who have the most grateful attitudes heal faster.

—Reprinted with permission from *Guideposts* magazine.

"One of the hardest acts of gratitude is to graciously accept a gift, to believe in the goodness of the person who gave it to us, and to believe in ourselves enough to receive it."
–Therese J. Borchard

Accepting gifts is harder than it might seem, especially if we feel unworthy. But our feelings of unworthiness can amount to a kind of ingratitude, just as failing to use the gifts we are given in this life is an insult to whomever or whatever created us. We have every right to be bold, and passionately grateful, as we accept our gifts and use them completely.

"Pain is a very precious gift. Do not waste it."
—Martha Singleterry

"No one is as capable of gratitude as one who has emerged from the kingdom of night."
—Elie Wiesel

"How far that little candle throws his beams! So shines a good deed in a naughty world."
—Shakespeare

On August 3, 1973, *The New York Times* published part of a letter that inmate Luis Vega wrote to the judge who sentenced him to serve a three-year sentence for selling and using drugs. The judge told the paper, "I get nasty letters, obscene letters, threatening letters, but this is the first time a thank-you letter for sending a guy to jail."

True gratitude requires honesty—with yourself, with the giver. Being thankful on a daily basis requires—and stimulates—a love for yourself and for the people around you. You can't be miserable and thankful about the same thing at the same time. Which sounds more fun?

Vega's letter reads, in part:

Since I been in prison, I been doing a lot of thinking about my own kids. And I wouldn't want them to go through the same thing I went through. And I pray that I can make life a little better for them.

So I feel that you have given me a chance to live and make it better for them.

Sir, at first, I hated you for sending me away. But then I understood what has to happen. So, I started to face it. And now I feel that all you did was to give me time to find myself and get together. So that when I go home, I can start a new life. And I wouldn't have to take drugs to keep me going.

This is why I'm writing this letter to you, to thank you. And my kids also thank you.

"Every problem has a gift for you in its hands."
—Richard Bach

We all find ourselves struggling in the midst of hard times. For me, even though I've been lucky, those hard times can be the true tests of my gratitude. It's easier to be thankful for cake and icing than for dry bread, but the bread is probably more sustaining in the long run, and will certainly give me added incentive to savor the sweeter things when they come my way. We can always seek and find a hidden gift of gratitude, even (or especially) in our darkest moments.

From a letter to *The New York Times*:

Perhaps mothers and fathers, before they grow into senility, should write a letter to their prospective caregiver, son or daughter, expressing gratitude for whatever decisions and actions they may, or may not, in the future, take in their long and painful process of being angels.

A thank-you letter in advance might ease the torment of one's beloved offspring. I will now do that, thanks to the perspective [this article] gave me.

Malka Z. Kornblatt
Boca Raton, Fla., Nov. 29, 2008

Thank you for listening.

"With the gift of listening comes the gift of healing."

–Catherine de Hueck

Thank you for trusting me.

"To be trusted is a greater compliment than being loved."

–George MacDonald

Thank you for your honesty.

"What is uttered from the heart alone, will win the hearts of others to your own."

–Johann Wolfgang von Goethe

Thank you for treating me so well.

"What people truly crave is appreciation."
–William James

Thank you for being my friend.

"I have learned that to have a good friend is the purest of all God's gifts, for it is a love that has no exchange or payment."
–Frances Farmer

Thank you for everything you've given me.

"Among its other benefits, giving liberates the soul of the giver."
–Maya Angelou

Thank you for helping me change, thank you for accepting me.

"God, grant me the serenity to accept the things I cannot change, the courage to change the things I can, and the wisdom to know the difference."

–Reinhold Niebuhr

Thank you for your patience.

"All human wisdom is summed up in two words— wait and hope."

–Alexandre Dumas, père

Thank you for the opportunity.

"Each day comes bearing its own gifts. Untie the ribbons."
—Ruth Ann Schabaker

Thank you for believing in me.

"And even though I was fat and hopeless at games, which are very unacceptable things for a schoolgirl, I was happy and confident. That was quite simply because I had a mother and a father at home who thought I was wonderful. They thought all their geese were swans. It was a gift greater than beauty or riches, the feeling that you were as fine as anyone else."

—Maeve Binchy

"We always lived our life in a place of gratitude. But this has drawn us closer together."

—Lorrie Sullenberger, wife of pilot Sully Sullenberger, who safely landed US Airways Flight 1549 in the Hudson River in January 2009

We all try to keep in perspective the importance and miracle of the simple fact of being alive. That appreciation for life can sometimes feel a bit abstract, especially if we're going through a tough time or if we're slogging through our daily routine. A wake-up call is something that brings us a clearer picture of our own mortality, and it's often the reason people make huge life changes for the better. I'm not suggesting that anyone go looking for a near-death experience, but when we come close to tragedy, or even when it touches our lives in a painful way, we can at least try to appreciate the forceful reminder to reconnect to our love for life.

This op-ed piece appeared in *The New York Times* on April 26, 1987.

This is a thank-you letter to those who helped me stop. They gave me gifts beyond measure—the feeling of self-control, the elation of freedom from addiction, and self-esteem.

The only way I know to repay them is to tell all those who are about to give up smoking or thinking more about it because of increasing restrictions on where they may smoke that these gifts will be theirs soon. Beyond compare, they will outweigh any pleasure of smoking and the discomfort of giving it up.

—A. M. Rosenthal

"Gratitude is born in hearts that take time to count up past mercies."
—Charles E. Jefferson

"Gratitude is the most exquisite form of courtesy."
—Jacques Maritain

"Seeds of discouragement will not grow in the thankful heart."
—Unknown

When someone tells you no, you can't, that isn't done, it's not possible, what's your reaction? I'm ashamed to say that too often mine is to believe them. I redirect my energies, refocus my wishes and dreams within whatever limitation the outside world puts on me. In some ways this serves me well—I can "make do" with almost anything and can sometimes even make something out of nothing. But in other ways, I'm not giving credit to the power of dreams and inspiration, no matter how outlandish they may seem to anyone else. I never realized that thankfulness could inoculate me against discouragement, whether it's coming from outside criticisms or inner self-doubt. If someone tells me I'm not up to snuff, I can thank them. Feedback about what is lacking can point me toward filling in the gaps, and ultimately that will be an encouragement and not a setback. So, the next time someone or something threatens to shut down your dreams and aspirations, put up a little garden sign in your mind: those seeds of discouragement just won't grow here!

"Saying thank you is more than good manners. It is good spirituality."
—Alfred Painter

My grandma used to say that manners make the man, and usually what she meant was very straightforward: that you could take the measure of a person by how courteous they were. Beyond that, I think she knew that outward manners are a reflection of inner peace, wisdom, and self-respect, and that anyone who can maintain their dignity and carry themselves well, particularly under duress, must have a grounded spiritual core. That core enables further dignity and ever stronger gratitude.

"For each new morning
with its light,
For rest and shelter of
the night,
For health and food,
For love and friends,
For everything Thy
goodness sends."

—Ralph Waldo Emerson

"Gratitude is the
memory of the heart."

—St. Mary Euphrasia
(Rose Virginie Pelletier)

"When eating fruit,
think of the person who
planted the tree."

—Vietnamese proverb

"A friend is a gift you give yourself."

—Robert Louis Stevenson

Dear Julie and Sammy:

This might sound a bit crazy, but bear with me. When I was a kid, I spent a lot of time out in the garden with my dad, and I remember very clearly when I grasped the concept of a perennial flower or plant. You only had to plant it once and it would go through its life cycle, seeming to die off in late fall, gone forever like the others in the garden, but when the ground warmed up and the April showers returned, it would spring up again by itself in the same spot, all fresh shoots and blossoms. These seemed like magic plants to me, coming back again and again, familiar and the same and yet new with each cycle of the seasons. Your friendship feels like that to me, and with each passing year, I know the roots are stronger, and I feel so lucky to get to watch and be a part of the cycles of your lives. I feel like somebody gave me the gift of sisters (which for an only child is quite a gift), and you guys mean more to me than you know. Thank you for being my perennial friends.

With so much love and respect,
Addie

Chapter Four

Offering Thanks, Receiving Abundance

"For it is in giving that
we receive."

—St. Francis of Assisi

The more you give, the more you get. The more you put into something, the more you take away. I don't mean just in a traditional sense of making an investment of time and energy that pays dividends of one kind or another down the line. I'm all in favor of pouring your heart and soul into the projects and relationships that are most important to you. But, when there's something important for us to give, we never wait to be motivated by some promise of future reward. The giving itself is the reward, often even more so when we're not expecting anything in return. The same is true of giving thanks: the more of it we throw out into the world, the more gratitude and opportunity come soaring back to us.

When you feel you have nothing, give something away. It helps you remember how much you have. There is a Zen story about an old monk who lives very humbly in a simple shack. One day a thief comes to his house, and instead of scaring the man away, the monk welcomes him enthusiastically as a guest, which of course is a huge surprise to the burglar. The monk has nothing to offer his guest, so he gives him the robe he is wearing, his only possession. The thief runs away, and the monk sits down to look at a beautiful full moon. What a shame, he thinks, that his guest could not stay long enough to enjoy the gift of seeing the moon.

"One must be poor to know the luxury of giving."
—George Eliot

Why is it that people who have almost nothing are willing to give away half of what they have to someone else in need, while many wealthier people would be hard-pressed to give away any significant percentage of their net worth?

"With every breath I take today,

I vow to be awake;

And every step I take,

I vow to take with a grateful heart—

So I may see with eyes of love

Into the hearts of all I meet,

To ease their burden when I can

And touch them with a smile of peace."

—Unknown

Open Letter to My Local Thief

Harry Fosha, New York Times, in Metropolitan Diary
by Glenn Collins
June 11, 1980

My Dear Thief:

I am quite sure you'll think that this is a letter of insult or, at least, of complaint. You are wrong. It is a thank-you letter.

First of all, I wish to thank you for giving meaning to a personal expression. I believe that you, my dear thief, are indeed "my thief"—just as I might refer to "my lawyer," "my banker" or "my sheriff." Why do I presume this to be true? Because, judging from what you carried away, I have no doubt that you could not in the same day visit somebody else.

I want to thank you, too, for something else: your sensitivity to sentimentality. Before your visit, I had two tape recorders: an old one, almost useless, but which I cherished for a lot of reasons; and a second one—new, of the cassette type, recently bought. I am grateful to say that, in ignoring the old machine, you left my memories untouched.

One favor please: could you send me a receipt for what you picked? (I would think that you know my address.) I believe that it might help to substantiate this theft, for tax and insurance purposes. You know how fussy those people from the IRS are.

Only a small complaint: When you departed, you left the window open. What carelessness. A thief could have come.

One-a-Day Thank-You Letters

Like eating an apple or taking a multivitamin or exercising, daily gratitude can improve your health, lower your stress, even change your life. I challenge you to write one thank-you letter a day for the next month. Thirty days—and they can be of any kind or manner. They can be out-of-the-blue thank yous, thank yous to people you don't even know, a couple of lines of quick thanks for a favor, a gift, an encouraging word. If you meet someone new at a party, send them a note right away. If you read about somebody doing work that you care about and think is important, write a thank you! Write to an author to thank them for a book that changed your life. I guarantee that by the end of the month you will feel more satisfied with your life. You may even manage to introduce yourself to new people, be offered new opportunities, or reap other rewards of your gratitude binge.

Thank you for the gift of this difficult time.

"Tests are a gift.
And great tests are a
great gift.
To fail the test is
a misfortune.
But to refuse the test is
to refuse the gift,
and something worse,
more irrevocable,
than misfortune."

—Lois McMaster Bujold

Thank you for helping me heal.

"We are all broken and wounded in this world. Some choose to grow strong at the broken places."

–Harold J. Duarte-Bernhardt

Thank you for the time we had.

"I still miss those I loved who are no longer with me, but I find I am grateful for having loved them. The gratitude has finally conquered the loss."

–Rita Mae Brown

Thank you for every little thing.

"Can you see the holiness in those things you take for granted—a paved road or a washing machine? If you concentrate on finding what is good in every situation, you will discover that your life will suddenly be filled with gratitude, a feeling that nurtures the soul."

—Rabbi Harold Kushner

"None is more impoverished than the one who has no gratitude. Gratitude is a currency that we can mint for ourselves and spend without fear of bankruptcy."
—Fred De Witt Van Amburgh

When I recently typed the words "thank you" into the online search engine Google, the first results that popped up were for a national bank's credit card rewards program. My heart sank. Even gratitude, it seems, can become a commodity, a reward, an incentive. That might be okay for a credit card, but when it carries into our personal relationships, we're in trouble. We have a growing cultural expectation of tit for tat in all things, which is frighteningly far removed from true thankfulness. If we reduce the natural rhythms of give and take to the status of a transaction in which we're always trying to balance out the equation or expecting something in return for everything we do, the end result will be disappointment.

We can all afford to practice the art of giving without planning to gain from it and being thankful right now, in the moment, without the prospect of future reward. The gift of being in the here and now will be its own reward program, I promise.

Your Giving List

The best way I know to shake off feeling that sense of entitlement, or tit for tat, is to rediscover the unbridled pleasure of giving. Sit down and make an expansive list of things you would like to give. Leave off anything you feel a sense of guilt or duty about; you can sort that out later. This is a list of purely joyful giving with no strings attached. Your list can include gifts to people you know and those you don't. It can include concrete things, like a book of poetry for someone you know would love it, to more intangible things like the gift of inspiration for a friend who's stuck in a rut. Don't limit yourself to things you think you can accomplish alone—dream big. If you would love to give someone their dream house, write it down. If you would love to give the world a peaceful solution to an international conflict, write it down. The more giving you can imagine and see in your mind's eye, the more connected you will become to your own giving spirit.

"Anything over and above your basic needs is sheer abundance, which is always close at hand. Abundance breeds gratitude, which in turn feeds more abundance. It's a win-win situation all around."
—Mina Parker

Ten simple and inexpensive ways to tune in to gratitude and abundance:

Take twenty dollars to a discount or dollar store and fill up two big bags of fun stuff.

Choose to go without. For a day or a week, eliminate something from your life—a favorite food, watching television, etc.—and appreciate it all the more.

Get outside to go for a hike, go camping, or even spend the day gardening. Seeing more plants and bugs and trees than you can count adds up to a concrete reminder of abundance.

Help someone less fortunate. Drive a senior around town to do their errands, volunteer at an animal shelter, teach kids to play chess.

Collect all the change from around your house and take it to a coin counter. Then donate the lot.

Organize a clothing swap where everyone brings gently used clothing that they don't need and people give and take freely. Whatever's left can go to charity, and everyone goes home with a new wardrobe.

Fill a huge bowl to overflowing with fruit you love to eat and place it on your kitchen table.

Host a potluck dinner at your house where everybody brings their favorite dish.

Bring a small gift to a child—a page of stickers, a box of watercolors.

Make a list of the people you are grateful for, and carry it in your pocket for a day.

"A hundred times every day I remind myself that my inner and outer life depend on the labors of other men, living and dead, and that I must exert myself in order to give in the same measure as I have received and am still receiving."

—Albert Einstein

"Anything that has real and lasting value is always a gift from within."

—Franz Kafka

"The gifts that one receives for giving are so immeasurable that it is almost an injustice to accept them."

–Rod McKuen

"This is the miracle that happens every time to those who really love; the more they give, the more they possess."

– Rainer Maria Rilke

Gratitude can inspire a sense of responsibility. It's always heartening to see someone take full advantage of the gifts they have been given. Everything we have today is a gift from those who have come before us. Think of the efforts of those people, of your ancestors, of the pioneers in your field. We have a huge responsibility to pass on all that and more to our children and their children, and to endow them with the knowledge that they have the power and privilege to live up to their potential. That kind of gratitude creates an ever-renewing cycle of abundance.

"Make all you can, save all you can, give all you can."

—John Wesley

"Purchase not friends by gifts; when thou ceasest to give, such will cease to love."

—Thomas Fuller

When we purchase friends with love, the gift returns itself again and again. Then our gifts to them are icing on the cake. And when we have no gifts to give, we will always have more love to give, and it will always be accepted enthusiastically.

"Every gift from a friend is a wish for your happiness."
—Richard Bach

Thank you to my friends,

who bring me joy in common and exceptional ways

who are there when I need them

who put up with me when I'm a pill

who give me advice when I need it most

who remind me to listen and to understand

who challenge me and grow with me

who make me laugh until I cry

who give me hope when I'm disheartened and courage when I'm afraid

the gift of their friendship fulfills every wish for happiness.

"Be silent as to services you have rendered, but speak of favours you have received."
—Seneca

Anonymous giving is a thrill. There is such enormous satisfaction in standing back in the shadows, knowing that your gift and the receiver are the focus of all the attention. Let the giving itself be the main event.

"I thank you God for this most amazing day, for the leaping greenly spirits of trees, and for the blue dream of sky and for everything which is natural, which is infinite, which is yes."

—e. e. cummings

"When you are grateful, fear disappears, and abundance appears."

—Anthony Robbins

"I think the dying pray
at the last not please
but thank you as a
guest thanks his host at
the door."

—Annie Dillard

"Be thankful for the least gift, so shalt thou be meant to receive greater."
–Thomas à Kempis

Gratitude multiplies through awareness. When we take the time to notice even the smallest things and recognize them as gifts—a prime parking spot, a phone call from a friend, some quiet time alone—then we invite more and greater gifts into our lives. We are all meant to receive great gifts, and keeping our eyes and hearts open to them ensures they won't pass us by.

"The most precious gift we can offer others is our presence. When mindfulness embraces those we love, they will bloom like flowers."
—Thich Nhat Hanh

It's the simplest gift we can give, and the most powerful: being there. I heard a speaker talk about fatherhood once, and he challenged the idea of spending "quality time" with your kids and suggested instead "quantity time." Quantity time is that time spent doing nothing and everything: changing diapers, making food, hanging out, and just being there in a way that doesn't have the pressure of time that has to be spent doing something important. I like applying the idea of quantity time not only to parenting but to other parts of my daily life. I can imbue everything that I do a lot of every day (working, driving, talking, cleaning) with a sense of just being in the moment and doing it rather than doing it to get it done and move on to something else.

"Love's gift cannot be given, it waits to be accepted."
—Rabindranath Tagore

To me, saying thank you is about accepting. It's about knowing you're worthy of the gift. It's about releasing the expectation that you have to do something or be something more than you are to be worthy. It returns the love that is offered with an open and thankful heart. It reflects the natural rhythms of give and take in the universe. It completes the circle.

Thank you, thank you, thank you.

"Gratitude is not only the greatest of virtues, but the parent of all others."

—Cicero

About the Author

Addie Johnson grew up in Minnesota and San Francisco, went east to Vassar College, and then stayed put in New York. She's an actor and helps run Rising Phoenix Rep, a small developmental theatre company. She's also an editor and writer, known for *The Little Book of Big Excuses*, *Lemons to Lemonade*, and *A Little Book of Thank Yous*. She lives in Brooklyn with her family, who help her remember every day that life is sweet.

Mango Publishing, established in 2014, publishes an eclectic list of books by diverse authors—both new and established voices—on topics ranging from business, personal growth, women's empowerment, LGBTQ studies, health, and spirituality to history, popular culture, time management, decluttering, lifestyle, mental wellness, aging, and sustainable living. We were recently named 2019 *and* 2020's #1 fastest growing independent publisher by *Publishers Weekly.* Our success is driven by our main goal, which is to publish high quality books that will entertain readers as well as make a positive difference in their lives.

Our readers are our most important resource; we value your input, suggestions, and ideas. We'd love to hear from you—after all, we are publishing books for you!

Please stay in touch with us and follow us at:

Facebook: Mango Publishing
Twitter: @MangoPublishing
Instagram: @MangoPublishing
LinkedIn: Mango Publishing
Pinterest: Mango Publishing
Newsletter: mangopublishinggroup.com/newsletter

Join us on Mango's journey to reinvent publishing, one book at a time.

CPSIA information can be obtained
at www.ICGtesting.com
Printed in the USA
JSHW031913310721
17425JS00002B/2